EMB[barcode] G

THE

PRESENT

LIVING
AN AWAKENED LIFE

LEONARD JACOBSON

A CONSCIOUS LIVING PUBLICATION

Introduction

In 1981, I experienced the first of a series of spontaneous spiritual awakenings that would radically alter
the course of my life. This first awakening lasted in
full intensity for a period of about three weeks and I
remained in an altered and awakened state of consciousness for about three months. During this first
experience, I was taken on a journey into other realms
of existence which resulted in my healing at a very
deep and personal level. It was revealed to me where
I had been hurt and damaged in my childhood and
where I had gone astray. It was as though I was being
guided back into the truth of life after being lost for
many lifetimes. At the very peak of this awakening
experience, I encountered the living presence of God.
To my utter amazement, I discovered that God was
completely without judgment. God was an allowing
God who filled my whole Being with an overwhelm-
ing sense of unconditional love and acceptance. I
spent many days intoxicated with love and a sense of
wonder and perfection. After about three months, the
experience ended and I was returned to who I had
been previously. This was completely unacceptable to
me and so my journey as a seeker began in earnest. I
explored many of the spiritual and mystical paths
and traditions. I was attracted to the teachings of the
Eastern Masters, Zen, the Sufis, the Taoists, the
Native Americans and some of the Western Mystics.
Gradually I found my way back to that awakened
state which I had experienced several years earlier.

Introduction ....

Grounded in a higher consciousness, I began teaching others how to awaken into love and the truth of life.

At the conclusion of a seven day retreat in 1984, without any warning or hint that it was coming, I experienced the second awakening. It was a chaotic and difficult journey which involved entry into a number of different dimensions at the same time. At first, I was immersed deeply into the eternal dimension of life. I existed completely outside of time. I felt like Adam, the first man. Everything I saw was filled with the divine presence of God. I was in a state of total silence, fully present and overflowing with love, wonder and amazement. This lasted for about a week. Suddenly, I found myself on the cross. I was Jesus being crucified. It was not a vision. I was actually there as Christ on the cross looking out through the eyes of Jesus. I experienced each moment of the crucifixion in perfect detail. Several times, I was taken from the cross to a higher divine realm where the truth about Jesus was revealed. The most disturbing aspect of this was that there were some very distinct differences between what I was experiencing on the cross and the Christian version of events as reported in the New Testament. When this intense experience of awakening came mercifully to an end, I slept for three days. When I awoke, I was in an entirely new dimension. There was nothing left of me from the past. I was entirely without thought. I was alive and awake in the eternal present. For the next three weeks, I lived in what I can only describe as Heaven on Earth.

Introduction ....

And then something deep within me stirred. I had the sense that I must emerge from this exalted state and re-enter the world of time. What I had experienced was to be shared with others. I resumed my teaching and for the next three years, I went through a complex and difficult process of integration. In January of 1991, I went through a third awakening which was more powerful than the previous two and almost ended in the loss of my physical life. It is beyond the scope of this book to go into a detailed description of the third awakening. It is enough to say that it was a full awakening into God consciousness. I was taken on a journey through the mystery of existence. I became the rocks and the trees and the birds and the sky. I journeyed through time from the beginning to the end and from the end to the beginning.

There have been four more awakenings since then and my life has been a gradual process of integration. I have been learning how to integrate the consciousness of God into everyday life.

As I share the Way with others, it becomes simpler and more precise. I am often astonished by how easy it is for others to awaken, provided that the True Way is revealed to them. Even then, it is a question of their readiness and their level of commitment. Full awakening does not come without paying a price. Unless awakening is the first priority in your life, it will not happen. There are hidden traps and pitfalls all the way along the path. It requires a great deal of alertness and vigilance to complete the journey.

Introduction ....

I have written three books which I trust will be of assistance to those who are ready to awaken fully.
The first is *Words from Silence*. It contains much of the wisdom revealed to me during the first awakening.
Embracing the Present is the second book. It follows on from the first and contains detailed guidance for those on the path of awakening. The primary focus in this book is on how to awaken fully into the present moment and how to remain awake in the activities of daily living.
Bridging Heaven and Earth is the third in the series.
It is a profoundly mystical work and contains much of what was revealed to me during the second and third awakenings, including the truth about Jesus.
It has taken a great deal of trust and courage on my part to share my life and the message contained within these books so openly. I am very aware that what I have to say will be upsetting to many who are not yet ready to let go of their beliefs and yet it is their cherished beliefs which have held them in bondage for so long.
I invite you to read this book with an open heart.
It is time to awaken out of the bondage of the mind.
It is time to awaken out of illusion.
It is time to embrace the truth which exists within you but which is only available as you awaken into the present moment. Seek only the truth.
It will set you free.

There is no greater gift than the gift of Presence.

The importance of being present

There is much talk these days about
the importance of being present.
However, very few people can guide you
into a state of true presence without you
having to become dependent upon them.
My intention is to share with you
how to become fully present
and how to remain present
in a way that empowers you fully.
As you deepen into presence,
and as you awaken more and more into Being,
you will find that the abundance of
the present moment begins to fill you.
For the first time in your life,
you will feel truly fulfilled.
You will be released from the pain
and limitations of the past.
You will be released from fear
and anxiety about the future.
You will find that God begins to
participate in your life in a way
that you could never have imagined.
By bringing yourself present,
you are honoring God,
and so God will respond to you.
It is that simple.

God is

God is the One.
God is the One in the All.
God is Pure Consciousness.
God is Silent Presence.
God is the silent presence
at the very heart of all things.
God is in everything and everything is in God.
There is only one God.
God is real.
God is here now.
God is present.
Only when you are fully present
will you encounter
the living presence of God.

The tree is present

The tree is present.
The flower is present.
The cow grazing in the field is present.
The dog and the horse are present.
The lion and the deer are present.
The butterfly and the mosquito are present.
The rocks and the mountains are present.
Every grain of sand is present.
The ocean and the waves are present.
The sky in all its vastness is present.
Every cloud drifting by is present.
Where could they be other than present?
Can a leaf fall from a tree
other than in the present moment?
Can a bird sing its song
other than right here and now?
Everything in God's world is present.
Except for one thing.
You!

If you are not present,
then where are you?

There are always two possibilities
at any moment in your life.
Either you are fully present
in your breathing body,
relating moment to moment
to that which is actually present
or you are in the mind.
When you are fully present, you are
in a state of consciousness called Being.
You are here now.
You are experiencing the reality
of the present moment.
You are awake.
You are enlightened.
You know the truth of life.
You are in God's world.
When you are in the mind,
you have abandoned the present moment.
You have abandoned the truth and reality
of God's world for the illusory world
of your own mind.
Using the power of thought and imagination,
you have entered into the mind's world of
the remembered past and the imagined future.
When you are in the mind, you are not here now.
What you are experiencing is not real.

Two worlds

There are two worlds.
God's world.
The world of the present moment.
And mind's world.
The world of the remembered past
and the imagined future.
Both are vast.
But only one is real.

Mind's world

Mind's world is the world of the
remembered past and the imagined future.
It is a world of virtual reality.
Almost the whole of humanity
is lost in this world of virtual reality.
It is a world of illusion, but we have become
so deeply involved in it that we have
come to believe that it is real.
And we are so firmly locked into the belief
that the mind's world is real,
that the real world cannot enter.

It is not until you awaken and become
fully present that you will realize
that you have not been present.
It is not until you awaken
that you will realize that
you have been asleep,
dreaming that you are awake.

The mind

The mind is a computer
which stores all of your past experiences.
It contains within it everything which you
have ever experienced in this lifetime.
These past experiences give you
a sense of identity.
They give you a sense of who you are, but this
sense of who you are is based upon the past.
Not only does your mind contain
all the past experiences of this lifetime,
but it contains all the experiences
of all your past lifetimes.
It also contains within it the collective experience
of all the life forms which have ever existed
from the beginning of time.
The mind is an awesome instrument.
Enter into it at your own risk.
It is very easy to get lost.

Mind

Mind is a state of consciousness
into which you enter and in which you dwell.
It is a complex network of thought.
It is a finely woven web of collective memory.
It is a world wide web of human consciousness.
In very early childhood, you began the process
of programming the mind with your own personal
experiences, beliefs, ideas, concepts and opinions.
This personal mind which is built upon the
collective mind gives you a sense of who you are.
This sense of who you are is your ego.

When you are in the mind,
you are in the past or the future.
The one place you are not
is in the present moment.
Reality exists only in the present moment.
Therefore when you are in the mind,
what you are experiencing is not real.

Conjuring up the past

Scientists have conducted experiments
where they have probed and stimulated
certain sections of the brain.
The subject of the experiment
is returned to a past experience
which seems to be completely real.
The colors, the smells, the sounds
and the sights are all experienced as real.
The feelings or emotions of the original experience
are fully recalled and relived as if they are real.
This means that when you are in the mind
you can regress to a past experience without
even realizing that you have done so.
Like a magician, you conjure up all the feelings
associated with that past experience
and then you project them
onto the present moment.
You believe that what you are experiencing
is real even though it is not.
It is all an illusion which you are projecting
from the past onto the present moment.
You are creating your own world of illusion.

Strategies of the ego

From a very early age,
the ego begins to develop within the mind.
The hurt and isolation is too much for you
to bear as a young child, and so the ego comes
into existence to help you deal with it.
It begins to develop strategies,
which enable you to avoid being hurt.
The ego is very effective,
and if you examine the strategies,
you will see that it has chosen the best course
of action, given the circumstances of your early life.
As you mature into an adult, however,
these same strategies are no longer appropriate.
They limit you and render you dysfunctional.
And yet, as long as they remain unconscious,
they will continue to dominate you.
Examples of these ego strategies are expressed
in the following sentences.
"I won't ask for what I want."
"I won't show my feelings."
"I will please others and ingratiate myself to them."
"I will rebel against others."
"I have to be recognized as the best."
"I will withdraw myself and then they can't hurt me."
"I will fill myself with anger and resentment
and then I won't have to feel the fear and the hurt."

Strategies of the ego ....

There are many more of these strategies,
most of which are designed to avoid hurt
and rejection or to gain you acceptance.
The ego is doing its very best to protect you.
But as the years pass, the ego becomes established
as the absolute ruler in the world of the mind.
It is in charge. It is in control.
And it loves the feeling of power and authority.
Its role gradually shifts from protecting you
to protecting itself and its position
as despot in the world of your mind.
You are imprisoned within the world of the mind,
and the ego is your prison guard
and your prison warden.
If you were to become more fully present, you would
begin to awaken out of the world of the mind.
The ego's position of authority would be threatened.
And so it develops a subtle and effective
set of strategies to make sure that you do not
become too present.
It is extremely skilled at tricking or seducing you back
into the world of the mind. Using a blend of fear,
judgment, desire and the promise of future fulfillment,
it lures you back into its world of the past and future,
where it is in control.
The ego does not want you to awaken,
for then it would have to surrender the throne.

How do you enter the mind?

You enter the mind by thinking.
Whenever you think,
you take yourself into mind's world.
It does not make any difference
whether it is a perfectly intelligent thought
or a profoundly spiritual thought.
All thinking has the same effect.
It takes you into the mind's world.
A world of the remembered past
and the imagined future.
A world of thought and belief.
A world of opinion and concept.
A world of memory and imagination.
A world of idea and abstraction.
A world of illusion.
If you want to come out of the mind,
then thinking will have to stop.

If you are thinking, then you are in the mind.
It is a simple test.

Not one thought you have is the truth.
So why bother thinking?

You would be quite amazed
to know how little I think.
I am not trying to stop thinking.
I think when it is necessary to think
but beyond that, I don't think.

You cannot think about the present.
You can only think about the past or the future.

You can choose to think

You can choose to think.
You can remain present as you think.
The fact that you are thinking is real.
What you are thinking about is not.

Unintended thinking

If you are thinking
but you are not intending to think,
then the mind is thinking by itself.
The mind is thinking itself into existence.
When your mind thinks by itself,
then you are caught in its world.
You cannot escape.
You are a prisoner of your own mind.

The walk

A man went for a walk one day.
As he walked, he became aware
that he was feeling lost and alone.
Rather than push the feelings away,
he allowed them to be present with him.
"I'm lost. I am all alone," he cried to himself.
A deep sadness arose within him.
Suddenly a voice arose from a deeper level.
"If you are lost, then where are you?"
It was the voice of his Being.
It was the voice of truth.
The man paused to consider the question.
"If I am lost, then where am I?" he asked aloud.
He sat down and as much as possible,
he stayed with his feelings.
"I am lost. I am all alone!"
he repeated several times.
Once again the voice of his Being
gently challenged him.
"You say you are lost. Then where are you?"

The walk ....

The man tried to see where he was.
Suddenly, it became clear to him.
"I am lost in my mind!" he cried.
It was so simple.
He was lost in his mind.
He was lost somewhere in his remembered past.
Or somewhere in his imagined future.
One thing was clear.
He was not here now.
He closed his eyes and became very still.
He became very aware of his body and his breath.
He became very aware of the sounds around him.
He could feel the soft caress
of the breeze upon his face.
He became silent.
He began to feel very present.
The feeling of being lost and alone disappeared.
He paused for a few moments in silent gratitude.
He opened his eyes and his heart exploded with joy
as a bird soared into the sky.

Watching the mind

If you want to escape
the tyranny and bondage of the mind,
then you will have to become very watchful
of what your mind is doing.
Don't be against the mind in any way.
Just see it for what it is doing
and what it is creating.
You cannot stop it.
All you can do is watch it
and somehow see through it.
You have to find a way of relating to your mind
in such a way that it knows that you see through it.
This is what it wants.
It will keep testing you until you arise in mastery
and it can no longer deceive you or fool you.
It is very subtle.
It needs to know that you see through it.
But if you try to stop it, it has beaten you.
It knows that you are not the true master,
for the true master would never try to stop it.
It is against the nature of the true master.
Unless you arise in mastery,
the mind will not release you.

A gentle remembering

The only thing which will help you
to get out of mind is gentle remembering.
With gentle remembering, you can bring yourself
into relatedness with that which is actually present.
You can tune into that which is here now with you.
Mind's world is the world of the past
and the future.
It cannot directly encounter
that which is actually present.
The mind cannot enter into the present moment.
So all you have to do is bring yourself into direct
relatedness with that which is actually present
and you must come out of the mind.
You must become present.
You must enter the world of Being.
There is no other possibility.

Remembering the present

In choosing the reality of the present moment,
you must do so without any judgment.
There can be no hint of rejecting the mind
or anything within mind's world.
The desire to transcend the mind
is a form of judgment.
And judgment is a test which you must not fail.
Simply recognize that you have been thinking.
Know that by thinking, you have taken yourself
into the mind's world of the past and the future.
Bring consciousness to that simple fact.
And then bring yourself present with that
which is actually here now.
Bring yourself present
with the tree which is in front of you.
Encounter its presence.
Hear the sound of the birds singing.
Feel the coolness of the air upon your face.
Smell the fragrant scent of the flowers.
Bring awareness to your breathing body.

Remembering the present ....

It is a gentle remembering.
You are not trying to stop thinking.
You are not trying to escape from the mind.
And so the doorway to Being
will be opened for you.
A total absence of judgment is the key
which unlocks the doorway to Being.
You are simply remembering to focus
on that which is present.
You are free to make that choice.
If the thoughts of the past and the future disappear
as you focus on that which is present,
then that is God's business.
You are innocent.
You were not seeking that.
It just happened.
If your mind falls completely silent,
then just relax into the silence.
Enjoy all that God has to offer you in this moment.
Enjoy the fullness and abundance of this moment.

A trick of the mind.

Whenever the thought arises that you want
to be more present and less in the mind,
then you must ask where
that thought is coming from.
Where is the desire to escape
the mind coming from?
It is coming from your mind.
It is the mind saying that
it wants to get out of itself.
But that is impossible.
Mind can not get out of mind.
It cannot leave itself.
It cannot become something other than mind.
It is extremely subtle.
It is a trick of the mind designed
to keep you in the mind.
The desire to escape from the mind
will take you further into the mind.

Neither for nor against

You can think but do not become identified
with what you are thinking about.
Do not take a position for or against
whatever it is that you are thinking about.
The moment you become identified with
your thoughts, you are caught into the mind.
The moment you believe in your thoughts
as the truth, you are lost in the mind.

Beyond practice

All spiritual practice is a function of the mind.
It is still mind seeking to practice something
in order to get somewhere or to achieve something.
That is why the practice of meditation
will ultimately fail.
All spiritual practice will ultimately fail.
You cannot practice your way out of the mind.

Awakening to Being

Awakening to Being
is a process
of inner unfolding.
As you awaken,
the truth of life
is gradually
revealed from within,
and you become aware
of the presence of God
in everything around you.
You become aware
of the presence of God
within you.

A *two step path of awakening*

The path of awakening is simple.
It is like a dance with two steps.
The first step involves bringing yourself present,
deepening into presence and becoming
more grounded in presence.
In the first step you are awakening to Being.
You are awakening into presence.
You are learning the art of being fully present.
The first step is the easy part.
The second step is more demanding.
It is not difficult to bring yourself present.
The problem is that the mind
keeps reclaiming you.
It keeps taking you into the mind's world
of the past or future, whether you like it or not.
The only way to overcome this
is to bring full consciousness to the mind.
You must get to know every aspect
of your own personal mind or ego,
It is like building up an identikit picture
of yourself at the level of ego.
The ego can only control you when it is allowed
to function at an unconscious level.

A two step path of awakening ....

It must be brought into the full light
of consciousness.
Every day of your life provides
ample opportunity to accomplish this.
Just bring the consciousness of Being
to the dimension of you which is
mean, greedy, ungrateful,
manipulative, competitive,
dominating, judging,
controlling,
insecure, frightened,
needy, hurt, angry,
false, pretending, hiding,
projecting,
repressing,
or defending.
I am not saying to change
any of these qualities about you.
It is essential that you do not judge
yourself in any way.
Just see these qualities as they arise in your
daily living and in your interaction with others.

A two step path of awakening ....

Bring consciousness to these qualities
as they arise within you.
Identify them.
Own them.
Accept them.
Confess them.
"I see you.
I do not judge you.
I do not reject you.
I do not seek to change you.
But I want you to know that I see you."
Eventually you will get to a stage
when you know your own mind so well
that it will no longer be able to deceive you.
"I see you but I do not follow you.
You may co-exist with me but you are not the truth.
I am the truth. I am is the truth."
At the end of this process of awakening,
you will be a fully conscious awakened Being.
You will be an enlightened Being.
An enlightened Being is one
whose unconscious mind has been brought
into the full light of consciousness.

Right relationship

You will have to come into right relationship
if you are to awaken fully. You will have to
come into right relationship with your
thinking mind and your feelings.
You will have to come into
right relationship with your past.
You will have to come into right relationship
with others and with life. You will have to come
into right relationship with God.

A test of Being

How do you know
whether you are in your mind
or whether you are in Being?
There is a simple test.
If you are thinking, then you are in your mind.
It does not matter what you are thinking about.
There are no exceptions.
Any thought takes you into your mind.
It is that simple.
The test of Being is equally simple.
It is a test of silence.
Are you silent?
Is silence present within?
If there are no thoughts, then you are silent.
You are not trying to stop the thoughts.
You are simply present and witnessing
an absence of thought.
Silence is witnessing itself.

The simple truth

The simple truth is that there is no life
outside of this moment.
The life which you believe in
is nothing but an illusion
which you have constructed
in your mind using the power
of thought, memory and imagination.
It is not real.
Nothing outside of this moment is real.

Life

How much of your life as you know it
exists within mind's world?
The world of the remembered past
and the imagined future.
How much of your sense of identity
is based upon memory of past experience?
Who are you in the present,
without reference to the past?
What is life like in the present moment
without reference to the past or the future?

Truth

Truth exists only in silence.
Truth exists only in the present moment.
You will have to be silent and fully present
if you are to know the Truth.

Knowing the truth

If you try to place everything I say
into your pre-existing framework
of understanding, then you will
take yourself into the mind.
You will remove yourself
from the present moment
where the truth is known in silence.
You will enter into the mind's world
of the remembered past or imagined future.
You will be entering the world
of opinion, concept and belief.
And the truth is always beyond belief.
Just hear what I am saying.
Do not agree with me.
Do not disagree.
Just be still.
And know.

The Truth

You cannot receive the truth from me.
It is not mine to give.
It is not my truth.
It is not your truth.
It is The Truth.
It belongs to God
and it is equally available to all.
If you recognize the truth
that I am speaking,
it is because you know it from within.
I am just taking you
to that place within you
where the truth is known
and where the truth has always been known.

By invitation only

I can only engage with you
to the extent that you allow me
to engage with you.
It is your invitation which allows me
to share with you.
I cannot go where I am not invited.
I will not go where I am not invited.
To do so would be a violation of you
and in violating you, I violate myself.
And this I will not do.

Speaking the truth

I might be the one
speaking these words of wisdom.
But you are the one hearing them.
Speaking and hearing
are dual aspects of each other.
They are essential to each other.
The one speaking the truth
and the one hearing the truth
are equal in the eyes of God.
Both are participating equally
in the expression of truth upon the Earth.
In a perfect expression of truth,
the speaker and the hearer are One.

There is no journey.
There is no destination.
You are already here.

Being here

There are many people
who did not want to incarnate
into the egoic physical realm.
They would have preferred
to remain with the soul.
Or they wanted to ascend to spirit.
The last thing they wanted was a descent to ego.
And so they do not really want to be here.
It is a strong feeling that runs through their lives.
They spend their whole life resisting being here.
Their life is a kind of silent protest.
They refuse to participate in what is here.
They sometimes feel terribly alone and isolated.
They often pursue enlightenment as a way
to escape being here.
They believe that they will not have to
come back if they become enlightened.
It is difficult for these people to learn the
lesson which they were sent here to learn.
It is a lesson of acceptance.
It is a lesson about judgment.
But mostly, it is a lesson about being here.
It does not matter where they are
or which dimension they are in,
sooner or later, they will have
to learn how to be here.

You were born into a world
where no-one is present.
You entered the mind
hoping to find someone there.

It is important that the mind
sees through the nature
of its own dilemma.

Accepting ego

Many of the spiritual traditions tell you that when
you become enlightened, there will be no ego left.
They imply that enlightenment
will lead to annihilation of the ego.
This is unhelpful and very misleading.
The nature of awakened Presence
is love and acceptance.
There is no possibility of judgment or rejection.
If the idea that the ego is to be annihilated
enters into you, because you read it
or heard it spoken somewhere, it will result
in an impossible conflict within the mind.
You will be caught between the desire of the ego
to escape its limited existence
and the ego's fear of no longer existing.
Ultimately, the ego will never allow itself
to be annihilated, and so it will do everything
it can to distract you from being present.
And it is very skilled at doing this.
The ego has to be reassured that
you are not seeking to get rid of it.
As long as you seek to annihilate the ego,
you will never awaken.
You will never become enlightened.

The ego

The ego goes with you all the way
on this journey of awakening.
Even when you have experienced
the deepest levels of Being,
the ego is waiting on the sidelines,
ready to claim the truth of Being as its own.
You must be constantly alert and watchful.
If you are thinking about yourself or anything else,
then that is a clue that your mind is active
and your ego is involved.
The test of Being is silence.
When you are fully awake,
there is no commentator left to comment or report
on your spiritual progress or condition.
You are simply silent and fully immersed
in the moment of Now.
You must become very clear about when you are in
full Presence and when you have re-entered the mind.
If you are not absolutely clear about that distinction,
then the ego will become spiritualized.
Once the ego becomes spiritualized, you are lost.
It is very difficult to find someone
who can bring you back.

Co-existing with the mind

When you awaken, the ego will not disappear.
It is not supposed to.
Even when you awaken fully,
you will have to co-exist with the mind.
The attempt to stop the mind from thinking
takes you further into it.
It is a house dividing against itself.
You cannot try to stop the mind in any way.
It is one of the world's greatest dilemmas.
You know that you must awaken out of the mind.
You know that the truth lies not in the past
or the future but in the present.
But if you try to stop the mind,
you will become locked more deeply into it.
How do you resolve this dilemma?
How do you find your way out of the mind?
When you think about the future,
do not get too involved in the outcome.
When you enter the past,
know that it is not the truth.
It is just a memory.
Do not believe in it as the truth.

Co-existing with the mind ....

Do not take any of your thinking too seriously.
I am not saying to be dismissive of it.
Allow it its life.
Allow it its expression.
Allow it its beliefs and concepts.
But do not believe in any of it.
Co-exist peacefully with the mind
and the mind's world of illusion.
To be for the mind or against the mind
in any way is to believe in it.
And then you will be caught up in it.
You will become a part of the illusion.
The right way to be with illusion
is to be neither for nor against
the illusion in any way.
Just see it for what it is.
It is an illusory world
created through the power of thought.
You are the one thinking.
You are the one creating the illusion
with your thoughts.
Do not get lost in your own creation.

Only in this moment

If you are fully present in this moment,
then in this moment
and only in this moment,
you are a fully awakened Being.
If in the next moment,
you are caught in your mind,
thinking about the past or the future,
then you are no longer awakened.
The awakened state has gone.
Your enlightenment has disappeared.

A state of separation

When you enter the mind,
you separate yourself from the present moment.
You separate yourself from God.
You separate yourself from the true source
of love, power and wisdom.
When you enter the mind,
you enter into a state of separation.

Separation

The mind lives in separation.
It also lives with the hope that
it will overcome the separation.
But that is impossible, for the very foundation
of the mind is separation.
It cannot overcome it.
It wants peace and wholeness.
But it will never find it.
If you really look at the way you live your life,
you will see that almost everything you do
is driven by your need to avoid
the experience of separation.
Your quest for love and acceptance
is driven by the fear of separation.
Your desire to be in relationship
is driven by the fear of separation.
You control others.
You are nice to others.

Separation ....

You seek to please others.
You avoid others.
So much of your interaction with others
is driven by the fear of separation.
You need to know that some one is there for you.
You do not want to be alone.
You do not want to face your aloneness.
The more successful you are at avoiding
your aloneness, the more lost you are to the
possibility and potential of your own awakening.
You can never truly succeed in overcoming
separation at the level of mind.
The mind cannot be other than what it is.
It is separate.
Separation has its role to play in your journey.
Surrender into it.
It is separation which will ultimately
deliver you into Oneness.

Accepting separation

There is no way to overcome
separation at the level of mind.
Separation is the natural state of the ego.
Separation is in duality with Oneness.
When you accept the separation.
and allow yourself to experience aloneness,
you will begin to move towards Oneness.
Separation, once accepted,
will deliver you into Oneness.
It will return you to God.
To accept that you are separate does not
mean that you have to be isolated and alone.
It does not mean that you have
to live your life separately.
You can be living in a family

Accepting separation ....

or a community and still be separate.
To be separate has nothing to do
with being physically alone.
In fact we are not meant to live alone.
We are gregarious by nature.
To be separate simply means to be fully
with yourself in the present moment.
You are not caught up in the past or the future.
You are not entangled with others.
You have surrendered the desire
to find completion or wholeness in another.
You have accepted that you must return
to Oneness alone.

Separate yourselves!

Separation is an essential
first step towards Oneness.
You are hopelessly entangled in each other.
You are entangled in your past.
You are entangled in your future.
You are entangled in your relationships.
You are entangled in blame, guilt,
expectation, resentment and control.
You are entangled in the idea
that you can own and possess each other.
To separate yourself is to untangle yourself.
It is a return to the present moment.
It is a return to aloneness.
It is a return to Oneness.

The only way to overcome separation
is to stop seeking to overcome it.

Relax into the separation.
Accept that you are separate.
It will return you to the centre of your Being.
It will return you to the truth of who you are.

Only when you accept that you are alone
will you discover that you are not alone.

A walk along the beach

Next time you walk along the beach
or though the park or the forest,
try saying to the trees or the clouds or the rocks,
"I am separate from you.
I have separated myself from you.
I have separated myself from you
so that I may know you."
It is an acknowledgment of separation.
When you truly own and accept the separation
and when you truly accept your aloneness,
the feeling of separation will dissolve
and a sense of Oneness will arise within you.

When you awaken, you will find that
there was no separation to overcome.
It was all an illusion.

A world of duality

To enter the mind is to enter
the world of experience within time.
To enter the mind is to enter
into the past and future.
To enter the mind is to enter
into the world of duality.
You will have to learn the art of living
in balance within duality if you are to come
to an inner place of still and silent presence.
That inner place is at the very centre of your Being.
It is the doorway to God.

Duality

Everything at the level of mind
is experienced within duality.
There are no exceptions.
You cannot experience hot without cold.
Hot defines cold and cold defines hot.
They are essential to each other.
It is the same with long and short
and day and night.
Most of us have very little difficulty in accepting
the dual nature of hot and cold,
long and short
and day and night.
But we are not so at ease with the dual nature
of happiness and sadness, joy and pain
or Oneness and separation.

Duality ....

It is impossible to experience happiness
without first experiencing sadness.
It is impossible to experience joy
without experiencing pain.
It is impossible to experience Oneness
without experiencing separation.
They define each other.
They are essential to each other.
And yet most of us are at odds
with sadness, pain, and separation.
We cannot see that sadness
is the doorway to happiness.
Pain is the doorway to joy.
And separation is the doorway to Oneness.
We do not know how to live
in a state of balance within duality.
We have become accustomed to rejecting
one side of duality for the other.

Duality ....

In our ignorance, we are throwing
ourselves off balance.
We are removing ourselves from the centre.
We are locking ourselves into the very thing
we are seeking to avoid.
That which you reject always rises up to claim you.
If you reject sadness,
you will become locked into it.
Sadness will take you over.
Happiness will be refused entry.
If you reject pain, you will be denied joy.
If you reject separation,
you will never experience Oneness.
Such is the nature of duality.
We must learn the art of living
in a state of balance within duality.
It is essential if we are to awaken
into the truth of life.

The mind by its very nature is controlling.

When you are in the mind,
you will be both controlling
and you will be controlled.
It is essential to bring consciousness
to the patterns of control in your life
if you are to live an awakened life.

Control

There is a part of the human mind,
whose task it is to be in control of you
and everything and everyone in your life.
The controlling part of the mind has the task
of protecting you and keeping you safe.
Originally, its task was to protect you
against physical harm.
If you were experiencing physical pain,
or even if there was a threat of physical pain,
the mind would immediately
go into action to protect you.
At its most basic and primitive level,
it would respond to a real and present situation
of danger with a flight or fight response.
In the process of our evolution, however,
the controlling part of the mind
has learned to respond to emotional pain
or the threat of emotional pain
in the same way that it responds to physical pain.
It believes that emotional pain can hurt you
and so it tries to protect you.
It employs the same flight or fight response
to deal with emotional pain even though
your physical survival is not at risk.

Control ....

This flight or fight response to emotional pain
gradually develops into a pattern
of withdrawing or attacking.
If you develop a pattern of withdrawing
in response to a perceived threat of emotional pain,
you will become lonely and isolated.
If you develop a pattern of attacking, you will
become aggressive and sometimes even violent.
It is important to remember that when the mind
is dealing with emotional pain in this way,
it is not responding to a real and present situation.
It is basing its reactions upon old memories,
usually from childhood.
It is projecting the emotional wounds
and traumas of the past onto the present
and then it insists upon being in control of you
so that you will not be hurt.
As far as the controlling part of your mind
is concerned, you are still a helpless baby
or at best a defenseless and vulnerable child.
It must take care of you.

The mind has to be in control of you if it is going to keep you safe and keep you away from those painful feelings of separation.

If you want to free yourself from the mind
and live more in the present moment,
you will have to surrender
the patterns of control
in your life.

Surrendering control

To surrender the patterns of control in your life,
you will have to identify those patterns of control
without any judgment.
Just see them for what they are.
They are an inevitable part of life
at the level of mind.
They are a part of who you have been in the past.
You will have to go through a process of taking
full responsibility for these patterns of control.
Recognize them as they arise within you.
Own them.
Confess them.
Do not try to change them.
They are from the past.
The present moment is completely free of the past.
As you awaken into the present moment,
these patterns of control will simply disappear.
They will have no place in the present moment.
They will become irrelevant and unnecessary.
At the level of Being,
there is no need to be in control.
At the level of Being,
you exist in a state of surrender.
You are surrendered to the will of God.
You are surrendered to life.

Patterns of control

There are some patterns of control
which are obvious and easy to identify.
Angry, aggressive, bullying or dominating
behavior are all examples of overt patterns
of control.
They are an attempt to overwhelm another person
with strength, power and force.
This kind of control is based upon a strategy
that is intended to intimidate the other person
into submission so that the one controlling
can have his or her own way.
Criticism and judgment
are also overt patterns of control.
They are intended to belittle and diminish another
so that the other person feels smaller
and is therefore easier to control.
These patterns of control are learned in our early
childhood relationship with our parents.
But there are less obvious patterns of control
which were also learned in early childhood.
To be a victim is a pattern of control.
Feeling hurt by another is a pattern of control.
To feel hurt or to be a victim is essentially
a strategy of manipulation.

Patterns of control ....

If you are hurt or if you are a helpless victim,
perhaps your oppressor will feel sorry for you
and will eventually modify his or her behavior
towards you.
Perhaps your oppressor will see that you are
helpless and will come to your rescue.
Perhaps your oppressor will see how much
you are hurting and will repent
and give you what you want.
To be a victim is a strategy of control
originally designed to manipulate
your mother and father
into giving you what you want.
It did not work with mommy and daddy
and it won't work with anyone else.
It is not a very successful strategy.
You would be far better off to drop this strategy
and just ask for what you want
or state clearly what you do not want.
Blame is another obvious strategy
or pattern of control.
If I can make you feel guilty,
you are more likely to give in to my will.
It is the same with expectation and resentment.

Patterns of control ....

Not all patterns of control involve other people.
The need to know and understand
is a pattern of control.
The need to be right is a pattern of control.
The need to be in charge is a pattern of control.
The need to be the best is a pattern of control.
The need to have things your own way
is a pattern of control.
The need to know what is going to happen
in the future is a pattern of control.
In fact, patterns of control are deeply entrenched
into so many aspects of our lives.
Most of our lifestyle habits are patterns of control.
Conditional giving or accepting
is a pattern of control.
Withholding is a pattern of control.
The list could go on and on.
Examine your life carefully.
How much do patterns of control play a part
in the daily events of your life?
How much do patterns of control
deprive you of the experience of fullness
and freedom in your life?

Your mind does not want you to wake up
because if you wake up it will no
longer be in control of you.

The mind is a world of illusion
sustained through the power of belief.

You can have your beliefs.
Just don't believe in them.

The only sin is belief in your beliefs.

The truth is beyond belief.

The truth has no power
to penetrate into the world of belief.
Belief must surrender of its own accord
before the truth can enter.

Belief in your beliefs
leads to all kinds of abuse
in the name of your beliefs.

Surrendering belief

As you surrender belief
in your thoughts and beliefs,
the energy in the mind begins to diminish.
As it diminishes, you will find it is so much
easier to come out of the mind.
It is so much easier to be present.

Belief in God

Belief in God separates you from God.
God can only be known through direct experience.
And you will never have a direct experience
of God as long as you believe in God.

God is not a comforter

So many people turn to God
to ease their pain or end their suffering.
They turn to God for comfort and salvation.
But God is not a comforter.
You are in pain for one reason
and one reason alone.
You are not present.
You are choosing to be in your mind
and so you are disconnected from God.
You are disconnected from the truth of life.
You are the creator of your suffering.
God does not mind if you suffer.
God does not mind if you are in pain.
There is no other way to turn you around.
God will deliver any lesson that is required
to awaken you out of your mind.
God wants only one thing.
God wants you present.

Life is the classroom.
God is the teacher.

Who am I?

This question can be answered at many levels.
At the level of Being,
I am pure consciousness.
I am silent presence.
I am love itself.
But at the level of mind
I am so much more.
I am greedy.
Needy.
Competitive.
Judgmental.
Critical.
I am angry and I am hurt.
I am addicted to peanuts and chocolate and TV
and having the toilet paper unfold from the top
rather than the bottom of the roll.
I do not acknowledge others.
I want to put others down.
I feel unwanted.
Unloved.
Abandoned.

Who am I? ....

Criticized.
Judged.
I feel separate and alone.
I feel that I am not good enough.
Nobody cares about me.
I want everything my own way.
I want people to like me.
I am nice, even when I am full of rage.
I am afraid of intimacy.
I keep others at a distance.
I am not as good as others.
I carry wounds within me from the past.
I feel guilty.
I am full of regret.
I am anxious about the future.
I am afraid of snakes and spiders.
I don't trust others.
I'm suspicious.
I'm controlling.
I'm manipulative.
I'm stubborn.

Who am I? ....

I am full of judgment.
I feel superior.
I am opinionated.
I am jealous and insecure.
I want to be right all the time.
I am afraid of failure.
I want to be noticed.
I want to be admired.
I want to be the best.
I feel inferior.
I am angry.
I am bitter.
I blame others for my unhappiness.
I am full of rage.
I have expectations of others.
I am full of resentment.
I feel stuck.
I feel empty.
I am rejecting.
I am vain.

Who am I ?....

I am mean.
I am ungrateful.
I use others.
I am arrogant.
I repress my feelings.
I am sometimes dishonest.
I don't ask for what I want and then
I get angry when I don't get what I want.
I am always seeking an advantage for myself.
Do not think for a moment
that I am talking about me.
I am describing each and every one of us
at the level of mind or ego.
Until you are willing to own that
this is who you are at the level of mind,
then you will never be able
to awaken out of the mind.
You will never come to know
the truth of who you are
at the level of Being.

The truth will set you free

Own who you are
at the level of mind.
Identify it.
Express it.
Confess it.
There is no shame.
There is no guilt.
There is no judgment.
There is only the truth.
And the truth will set you free.

Projecting onto others

You project onto others
those aspects of yourself
which you deny and disown.
And then you have to live in a world
which is full of your own projections.
It is an illusory world of your own creation.

Only when you are fully present
will you live in the real world
which is free of your projections.

When you are in the mind,
you are essentially a projector.
Just like a movie projector, you project
so much of your disowned inner world
onto the outside world and onto others.
You project your disowned anger and hatred
and then you feel that the world is against you.
You project your disowned judgment
and then you feel judged.
You project your rejection of others
and then you feel rejected and alone.
You project events and feelings
from the past onto the present.
As long as you continue to project,
you will distort what is before you.
You will be seeing a reality distorted
by your own projections.
What you see in others is inside you.
It does not exist outside of you.
You have to own your projections.
Take them back.
Switch off the projector so that you can encounter
the truth and reality of the present moment.

Projecting onto the guru

You have to be very careful
when you become involved
with the Guru or the Master.
The guru understands that you are a projector.
It is not difficult for the guru
to dress himself up and create an image
and a mystique which will encourage
your projections onto him.
He makes himself a suitable screen
for your projections.
But he does not want your negative projections.
He is after your positive projections.
The source of love and truth exists
within each one of us.
The guru can encourage you
to project the source of love and truth onto him.
It is not difficult to manipulate your projections.
As long as you continue to project
the negative aspects of yourself,
you can be very easily manipulated
to project the positive aspects of yourself.

Projecting onto the guru ....

You can be manipulated into projecting
the source of love and truth onto the guru,
who is more than happy
to receive your projections.
In a way, the guru is empowered
by your positive projections.
There is nothing wrong with seeking out
a guru who can guide you into presence
and show you how to liberate
yourself from the mind.
But be careful.
Be watchful.
Make sure that the guru
is not seeking to establish himself
as the doorway to God.
Own all your projections.
Both the negative and positive ones.
They are yours.
Take them back.
Dare to be all that you are.

I do not want your projections

I do not make it easy for you to see me.
I don't dress myself up in any way
to encourage your projections.
If you are to see me,
then you will have to go to that level
within yourself where I am.
You will have to own all your projections
and become fully present.
Only then will you see me.
Only then will you know who I am.
And in that moment of knowing me,
you will know yourself.
For in truth we are one.
I am the One.
You are the One.
We are the One.

Whenever you see the love in me,
know that it is the love in you
that you are seeing.

Any fostering of dependency
by a teacher or a Master
is against the law of God.
No one has the right
to stand between you and God.
Not Buddha.
Not Christ.
Not anyone.

The Master

If to be a Master means to be a master
of my own mind, then I am a Master
in the true sense of the word.
But I am not your Master.
If in my presence
and with my guidance
you arise to inner Mastery,
then our coming together
has been worthwhile.

Beyond the Master and the guru,
I am.

We never truly meet other than in silence.
We never truly meet other than
in the present moment.

What I am saying is far less important
than you being present while I am saying it.

There is nothing to fear

There is nothing to fear in the present moment.
There is nothing to protect yourself against.
There is nothing to understand.
There is nothing to control.
It is only in the mind's world
of the past and future
that there is fear
and a need
for protection,
understanding
and control.

Being selfish

You will have to put yourself first
if you want to awaken.
The world will try to stop you from doing this.
You will be told that you are selfish.
It is a judgment which was imposed
upon you in early childhood.
It is a judgment which is intended to control you.
It is intended to stop you
from doing what you want.
It is an attempt to get you to do what others want.
Do not fall for this trap.
To put yourself first is not selfish.
To know what you want and to know
what you do not want is not selfish.
It is empowering.
Those who want to control you
do not want you empowered.

Becoming present

The only way to bring yourself fully present
is to become fully present with whatever
is actually here now with you.
If you can see it, hear it, feel it, taste it
or smell it, then it is here now with you.
It is present.
You honor that which is present
by being present with it.
The more you honor that which is present and
the more grateful you are for that which is present,
the more you will deepen into presence.

Honor that which is.
You are so lost in honoring that which is not,
that you forget to honor that which is.

There is only the present moment.
Be still and know.

To be present is to come out of time.
To come out of time is to come out of the mind.

A walk in the garden

Go outside and find a comfortable place
to sit in the garden.
Close your eyes and become very present
in your breathing body.
Become present with the sounds
you hear each moment.
Feel the warmth of the sun
or the coolness of the breeze.
Spend about five minutes becoming very present
and then open your eyes and begin to
walk slowly around the garden.
Become very present with everything you see.
Be present with a flower.
Then a tree.
Then another flower.
Be present with one thing at a time
and yet have the sense of the whole garden
being present with you.
Tell each flower and each bush and each tree
that you see it.
"I am here and I see you"

A walk in the garden ....

Say it many times to the trees and the flowers
as if they can hear you.
Say it to a leaf.
Or a branch.
Be very focused as you walk around the garden.
See everything in detail but without any thought.
You can tell the trees or the flowers
how beautiful they are if you want to.
You can say how much you love
and appreciate them.
Or you can remain silent.
The important thing is that you
are authentic and sincere.
Let them truly feel that you are present with them.
You are sharing the gift of presence with them.
And they are sharing the gift of presence with you.
Let it be a sacred experience.
If you are truly present during your time
in the garden, you will begin to encounter
the living presence of God.

Eating a meal

Close your eyes and become very present
in your breathing body.
Become very present with the sounds
you hear each moment.
Smell the food on the table in front of you.
Know that there is no life outside of this moment.
Feel the fullness of this moment.
Have a sense of gratitude for everything
that the present moment is offering you.
Now open your eyes.
See the plates, the glasses, the cutlery and
anything else which is on the table in front of you.
See the food.
Smell the food.
Hear the birds outside.
Be aware of the presence of the other Beings
sitting at the table ready to share a meal with you.
Pass the food or water to each other
very slowly and very lovingly.

Eating a meal ....

Let there be a sense of timelessness.
A sense of mystery.
And then, with a deep sense of gratitude,
begin to take the first mouthful.
Move your fork very slowly to the plate
and then very slowly to your mouth.
Taste the food as if you have never
tasted anything before.
Let it be the first mouthful of food in your life.
Savor each delicious taste.
Chew slowly and consciously.
Be fully present in your chewing.
Be fully present in every movement.
Be fully present in your sense of taste
and your sense of smell.
Be fully present in your hearing and your sight.
You will be amazed by the sacredness
of such an ordinary experience as eating a meal.
It will reveal to you just how unconscious your life
has been prior to this sacred occasion.

The only way you can acknowledge
the presence of God is to be present.

To be in a state of silent Presence
is to be in a state of true prayer.

Letting go

You cannot hold on to love.
You cannot hold on to truth.
Love and truth belong
to the present moment.
Surrender the love and truth
of this moment
and you will find
love and truth,
like two faithful friends,
waiting for you
in the next moment.

As long as you let love and truth go,
they will never leave you.

The ego wants to escape

The ego wants to escape from the
painful memories locked within the mind.
It wants to escape from the feelings
of helplessness, hurt and despair.
It wants to escape the feelings
of isolation and separation.
And so it will pursue enlightenment
in order to escape from itself.
It will practice meditation.
It will attempt to spiritualize itself.
It will create illusory experiences
of God and Christ to create an illusion
of comfort and salvation.
But it will fail.
It must fail.
For the ego cannot escape from itself.
It is impossible.
It must remain what it is.
It is one dimension of the whole
and it can never transcend itself.
If it wants relief from the pain and the despair,
then it will have to release you.
It will have to release you
from the past and the future.
It will have to release you into the present.
It will have to release you into Being.
It will have to release you into the One.

126

Unburdening the mind

I will share with you a secret that will
unburden your mind and set you free forever.
The feelings from which the mind is trying
to escape do not belong to the mind.
They have never belonged to the mind.
They have no rightful place in the mind.
The mind is personal.
It gives you a sense of personal identity
which is based upon the past.
Feelings, however, are impersonal.
They belong to God.
Do not personalize them.
Do not become identified with them.

Unburdening the mind ....

If feelings arise within you, then just feel them.
Allow them to be experienced within you.
They will pass through you.
They will not enter into you.
They will not become a part
of your personal identity.
If you are for or against the feelings in any way,
you will have personalized those feelings.
If you are for the feelings,
you will become attached to them.
If you are against the feelings,
you will repress them within you.
In either case you have taken
the impersonal feelings into your personal identity.
You have taken the impersonal into the personal.
And this you must not do.

Feelings

Feelings arise in the present moment,
even though what the feeling is about
comes from the remembered past
or the imagined future.
If you are fully present with the feelings
as they arise, then you will bring yourself
out of the mind and into the present moment.
If you become involved with what the feelings
are about, then you will be caught
into the mind's world once again.
If you judge or repress your feelings
you will be caught into mind's world.
If you project your feelings onto others,
you will be caught into mind's world.
If you disown your feelings in any way,
you will be caught into mind's world.
If you are for or against your feelings in any way,
then you will be caught into mind's world.
All you can do is feel your feelings as they arise.
Experience the feelings consciously as they present
themselves and they will pass through you
like a river flowing to the sea.

If you are to awaken, you will have to learn
how to be in right relationship
with your feelings.

Don't think your feelings.
Feel your feelings.

There is nothing you need to know

To analyze your feelings is to think your feelings.
It will take you out of the present moment
and into the mind.
If there is anything you are meant to know
about your feelings, it will be revealed
from within the feelings as you experience them.
And if nothing is revealed,
then just relax and feel the feelings.
There is nothing you need to know.

Anger and hurt

If you have anger arising within you,
allow the anger full expression.
I am not saying that you should express the anger.
I am saying that you should allow
the anger to express itself within you.
It is the same with hurt.
Feel the hurt but do not
get involved personally in it.
Just allow hurt to experience itself within you.
Allow hurt and sadness full expression within you.

Anger always arises in response to hurt.
If you allow yourself to feel the hurt,
you will not have to become angry.

Hurt

If you really allow yourself to feel
the hurt or the sadness,
the very worst that can happen
is that you will cry.
Let the tears flow.
Welcome them.
It won't be long before the tears turn to laughter,
and the pain reveals the joy hidden within it.

Anger

Anger is not polite.
It loves to swear and curse and threaten.
Anger is not logical or rational.
It hits and scratches.
It seeks revenge.
Anger is quite happy to inflict punishment
which is far greater than the crime.
Allow anger its full expression.
Just don't believe in it.
Do not become identified with it.
Do not blame anyone for your anger.
It is arising within you and it is yours alone.
It is coming from your past.
It is coming from your childhood.
It is an indication of your belief that you
cannot have what you want
or that you must accept
what you do not want
and you are angry about that.
You are very, very angry about that.

Anger ....

You have carried that anger
within you since early childhood,
and you blame all those in your life now
for not being able to have what you want.
You blame your wife.
You blame your children.
You blame your employer.
You blame the government.
You even blame God.
You are not getting what you want
simply because you believe that
you cannot have what you want.
That belief is programmed into your mind
at an unconscious level.
It is not until you bring it into
the full consciousness of Being
that you can begin to free yourself from it.
It is not until you take full responsibility
for that belief and stop blaming others for it,
that you can begin to live
an empowered life of freedom.

Hate

Hate is cold.
Hate is closed.
Hate is unforgiving.
Hate is anger which has become solidified.
Do not project your hatred onto others for it will
be reflected back to you just as your face is reflected
back to you whenever you look into the mirror.
Your hatred is arising out of an old wound
which has not yet healed.
It is arising out of a lifetime of unfulfilled needs.
When hatred arises within you,
let yourself be full of hate.
Enter into hatred's world.
Feel it. Own it. Express it.
But do not believe in it.
It is arising within you, but it is not the truth.
Only love is the truth.
Release the past by becoming present.
Let go of blame.
Surrender expectation and resentment.
Ask for what you want but do not
be attached to the outcome.
Take responsibility for your unfulfilled needs.
Slowly, hatred will begin to dissolve within you.
Anger and resentment will disappear
from your life.
Only love and the present moment will remain.

Hate

You are afraid to express your hatred.
Your hatred has been condemned
and driven underground
but it will not go away.
It lives its life within you,
hidden from view.
It even hides from you.
And then you don't know who you hate.
You don't know how much you hate.
At the deepest level, you even hate God.

Many people
will have to express
their hatred towards God.
It is hidden deep within them
and acts as an impenetrable barrier
to their love for God
which exists at a still deeper level.

A prayer of hatred

Say these words to God.
"I loved you God.
How could you do this to me?
How could you send me into the wilderness?
How could you send me into the darkness?
How could you deceive me?
I trusted you!
You sent me away from you
and now I cannot find my way back!
Why did you not warn me?
Why did you not come to my aid?
How could you let me suffer so?
I hate you for that!
I will never forgive you."
God will not judge you
or condemn you for your hatred.
God will love you for your confession.
For if you truly express your hatred towards God
it will open the door to your infinite
and unwavering love for God.

When you express your hatred towards God,
you will come to realize that
God accepts even that.

God is not a God of vengeance.
God has no judgment.
God allows.

Rage

I honor rage.
Rage is neither violent nor destructive.
It has no desire or intention to hurt anyone.
It just wants to be allowed full expression.
It is not wise to repress rage within you,
for to do so will turn rage into violence.
Rage is not meant to be acted out.
It is meant to be expressed responsibly.
It is meant to be declared.
Rage is a warning.
It is a warning to the whole world
not to interfere with you.
"Respect my boundaries," declares rage.
"Do not invade my space.
Do not interfere with me.
Do not judge me.
Do not try to control me.
Do not violate me.

Rage ....

Be warned.
Be afraid.
Be very afraid.
For I will deal with you harshly
if you do not heed my warning.
I do not want to harm you
but I will not allow you to interfere with me.
I am here and I have a right to be here.
It would be most unwise to stand in my way."
Allow rage to express itself within you.
Allow rage to enjoy itself within you.
Rage is your friend.
Do not condemn it.
Rage is impersonal.
In truth, rage is God
in one of God's purest forms.
Rage is God without any disguise.

The expression of anger and rage

Whenever I encourage you to express
anger or rage, I assume that you will
do so in a responsible way.
Do not involve any one else
in the expression of these feelings.
No one is to blame for your anger or rage.
You alone are responsible for these feelings.
It is better that no one is present when you
express these feelings unless those who are
present can allow you full expression
without getting caught up in any way.
The feelings are arising within you.
The expression of rage and anger
is between you and God and no one else.

That which you reject always rises up
to claim you as its own.

I will not allow you to destroy me

I exist in the present moment.
My life exists here now.
If you seek to engage me
into your mind's world,
then without realizing it,
you are destroying me
and you are destroying my life.
You are trying to take me
into your past or your future
and I will not allow it.
If you persist, then I will leave you,
and if I cannot leave you,
then beware!
I will become enraged.

A difficult journey

It has been almost impossible
for me to escape from my mind's world.
It has been a difficult journey to escape
from the entanglements of my own past.
What hope do I have if I am caught
in your mind's world.
How can I untangle myself from your past?
How can I untangle myself from
your expectations,
your fear,
your anger,
your hurt,
your blame,
your guilt,
your childhood wounds
and unfulfilled needs.
These things belong to your past.
Not mine.
You have no right to take me there.
Untangle yourself.
Come out of your mind.
Be present with me.
Remind me to be present with you.
Free of the past, let us share
the present moment together.

If you want to awaken into true power,
you will have to awaken into the present moment.
You will have to awaken into Being.
True power is a dimension of God.
It is a dimension of the One.

God does not just want Beings of love.
God wants powerful Beings of love.

True power

At the level of mind, we feel powerful when we
are in a position of strength or power
in relation to others.
We acquire the feeling of power when we are able
to impose our will over someone else.
True power, however, is not in relationship
with anyone or anything.
The moment you take power into relationship,
you have assumed power over someone.
Someone is now a victim to your power.
You have taken power into the mind.
You have taken power into duality.
Because you have taken power into duality,
you will now have to experience power
in its dual state.
Sometimes you will be more powerful than others.
At other times you will be less powerful
than others.
Sometimes you will be the abuser of power.
Other times you will be abused by power.

True power ....

This can occur within one lifetime
or it can occur over many lifetimes.
One lifetime you will be the abuser.
The next lifetime you will be the abused.
This will continue until you recognize that
true power is an attribute of God
which exists within you and has
nothing to do with anyone else.
True power is impersonal.
It is of the One.
It is a dimension of God.
It cannot be owned.
It cannot be personalized.
It cannot be used to gain for yourself an advantage
or a position of power over anyone or anything.
True power will empower you
in the present moment.
It will bring you into the fullness
and the vitality of life.
It will fill you with the presence of God.

You are in a state of true power
when you know what you want,
when you know what you don't want
and you can express both clearly
without any attachment to outcome.

Anger is a sign of powerlessness

Anger is a sign of powerlessness.
Underlying anger is the belief
that you cannot have what you want
or that you must put up
with what you do not want.
And you are angry about that even if you keep
your anger repressed and hidden
from yourself and from the world.
These beliefs are rooted in the past.
They were established in your childhood
relationship with your parents.
They were true then but they are no longer true.
You will have to come out of the mind
to free yourself from these old beliefs.
You will have to come out of the past.
You will have to awaken into the present
which is completely free of the past.

A return to power

You came into the world
as a fully empowered Being.
Although you were just a tiny baby,
you knew exactly what you wanted,
you knew exactly when you wanted it
and you knew exactly how to ask for it.
A little cry and mommy
was supposed to produce the breast.
A little murmur and mommy
was supposed to pick you up
and hold you in her arms.
A little wriggle and mommy
was supposed to put you down.
As you grew older, you exercised this power
with great authority as though you were
the only Being in the world.
You were entitled to have whatever you wanted.
You were entitled to do whatever you wanted.
But mommy and daddy had a different view.
They believed that they had a right
to a life of their own.
And so a battle of wills developed.
You were a worthy adversary.
The temper tantrum was one of the
finest weapons in your arsenal.

A return to power ....

You were much more powerful
than your parents but they were bigger.
Eventually they won.
Their will prevailed over yours.
You accepted defeat.
You surrendered the absolute certainty
that you can have and do whatever you want.
You gradually arrived at the belief
that you would have to live according
to the demands and expectations of others.
You would be guilty if you resisted.
You would be cast out.
You would be banished.
You would be alone.
Gradually you learned the art of living
in their world.
A world of the mind.
A world of thought and opinion.
A world of concept and belief.
A world of expectation and resentment.
A world of blame and guilt.
A world of control and ownership.
A world of hurt and anger.

A return to power ....

It has been a difficult and painful journey
into an illusory world.
It is time to return to the real world.
It is time to remember who you are.
You are a Being of love.
You are an empowered Being of love.
You can have whatever you want.
You can do whatever you want.
The only difference between the empowered
state now and your empowered state as an infant
is that you have come to recognize that others
have the same rights as you.
You can no longer impose your will upon others.
You also recognize that what you want
is always changing so you are no longer
attached to the outcome.
It has been a long and difficult journey
to arrive at such a simple conclusion.

One who is truly empowered
would never interfere with another.
One who is truly empowered
would never seek to control another.
One who is truly empowered
would never assume responsibility
for another.

True responsibility

True responsibility exists within your recognition
that every choice and every decision you make
and every action you take leads inevitably
to the consequences which follow.
Whatever you are experiencing in your life right
now is directly attributable to some earlier choice
or decision you have made in the past.
Learn how to connect the dots and you will be free.
This means connect the choice or the decision
made by you in the past with the consequences
which you are currently experiencing.
Take responsibility for your choices and decisions
and see that you are creating everything
that is happening in your life now,
whether it is positive or negative.
Once you truly understand and accept this,
you will have entered into true responsibility.
You will have put an end to blame, guilt, control,
expectation and resentment in your life.

Thoughts are creative

Thoughts are creative, but for most people,
thoughts and beliefs occur at an unconscious level.
On the surface, you might want a new job
or a partner to share your life with.
You might pray for these things to appear
in your life and yet they do not.
This is because, at an unconscious level, you
are harboring contradictory thoughts and beliefs.
For example, at an unconscious level,
you might believe that you are not good enough
or that you are unwanted or unloved.
These unconscious thoughts and beliefs
are in direct conflict with your conscious thoughts
and so life does not know how to respond to you.
More than likely, your unconscious thoughts
will prevail.
It is necessary to bring these unconscious thoughts
and beliefs into consciousness and replace
them with clear and creative thought.
Then what you think will manifest in your life.
But not always!
The power of creative thought
is subject to a higher law.

Thoughts are creative ....

Ultimately, the law of Karma prevails
over your conscious thoughts and desires.
Prior to your current incarnation,
you existed at the level of soul,
and one of your principal objectives
in incarnating into this lifetime,
was to heal and purify past Karma
which is affecting the soul.
You came here to learn lessons about
love, acceptance, power and compassion.
You came here to awaken into love,
truth and Oneness.
You came here to deliver your own soul
into the conscious experience of Immortality.
And so, the script of your life was written prior
to your incarnating into physical form.
It was intended to give you the highest opportunity
to awaken and learn your lessons.
In other words, it does not matter what you want.
What will ultimately emerge in your life is
whatever is for your highest good,
and that is largely predetermined
by the soul's script and the law of Karma.

Thoughts are creative ....

There is an even deeper level.
Everything that occurs in your life
is a part of God's plan to wake you up
and bring you fully present.
We are so fast asleep that sometimes
God has to shake us up to wake us up.
Whatever it takes!
Once we are fully present, then we are
fully conscious and awakened Beings of Love.
We know who we are and we know God
and we are awake in the truth of life.
We come to see that God has already created all that is
and we relax into the perfection of that.
There is no need to create anything ourselves.
At this level, we begin to experience Heaven on Earth
and our true and most perfect future unfolds
through the doorway of the present moment.
It is inevitable.
This is a rare state of attainment,
but it is our ultimate destiny.

A day by the lake

The other day I was sitting
beside a lake and some ducks
swam up beside me.
I was flooded with love for them.
I found myself referring to them as my children.
My beautiful, perfect, divine children.
And my paternal feelings do not end there.
I often think of my dog as my child.
And the horse in the paddock next door
is another one of my children.
All of God's creatures are my children.
And all of your children are my children.
You do not own them.
They are as much mine as yours.

The True Mother and the True Father

Awakening to Being will herald the arrival
of the True Mother and the True Father.
We do not know who they are yet.
We do not know what they will be like.
We only know the false mother
and the false father.
We have all been raised by the
false mother and the false father.
It is not their fault.
No one is to blame.
But the time of the True Mother
and the True Father is approaching.
If we can acknowledge that we have been
the false mother and the false father,
then we open the way for the birth
of the True Mother and the True Father
within us.

In the beginning

When we came into the world,
we were fully awake little Beings
in frail and vulnerable bodies.
We were totally present and innocent,
but the world we had been born into
was full of people who lived almost
exclusively in the world of the mind.
Very few people, including our parents,
could meet us and relate to us at the
level of consciousness that we existed at.
We were fully present little Beings.
In order to feel safe and overcome
the trauma of separation that we endured
during the birth process, we needed the
unconditional love of one who is fully present,
But the love and acceptance we received
was conditional.
No one, including our parents,
knew how to be truly present with us.

In the beginning ....

And so we felt alone and isolated
at a very subtle level.
We were faced with being the only one
in our world who was fully present,
and at such a young age, that was intolerable.
We could not bear the aloneness of it.
By the age of four, we had joined our parents
in their world of the mind.
We partly chose it, rather than remain alone,
but also we were conditioned and coerced into it.
Then began the long and arduous process of
learning how to survive and thrive the world
of the human thinking mind.
Some of us succeeded and some did not.
Those of us who failed are the fortunate ones,
for we suffered, and it is our suffering
that provides the motivation to look within
and find our way to the truth of life.

What a child really needs
is a mother and a father who are truly present.
Only parents who know how to be fully present
can give the child what it really needs.
No one should be allowed to have children
until they have completed a course
in the art of being fully present.

The caretakers

You are the caretakers of your children,
so you have a responsibility to take care of them.
You have a responsibility to provide
food and shelter for them.
You have a responsibility to protect them
and make sure that they are safe.
You have a responsibility to welcome
them into the physical world.
But above all, you have a responsibility
to be present with them.
If you are truly present with them,
then all their needs will be met.
Simply by being present with them,
they will experience unconditional
love and acceptance.
They will experience a world
which is safe and welcoming.
They will experience a life
without judgment, guilt or blame.

The baby in the restaurant

I was sitting alone in a restaurant
in New York City.
A couple walked in and sat down
at the table next to mine.
They had a young baby with them.
She was a very beautiful child
about twelve months old.
I was struck by the loving and caring
energy of the mother and father and
the strong presence of the child.
Occasionally the child's eyes
would meet mine and we remained
for some time in silent communion.
They had some slices of lemon
on their table, probably meant for the tea
which the parents were drinking.
The baby had picked up one of the
slices of lemon and was sucking on it.
She had all the facial expressions
you would expect of a baby sucking on a
slice of lemon, but she seemed to be enjoying it.

The baby in the restaurant ....

The parents were concerned that the lemon
was too sour, so they tried to coax her into
surrendering the lemon by offering
her some ice cream.
"A perfectly reasonable offer,"
I thought to myself.
But the child preferred the lemon.
The parents persisted until their will
prevailed over that of the child.
The lemon was removed
and the ice-cream substituted.
I watched on in fascination.
I could not believe the strength and will
of the young child.
She was so clear about what she wanted.
It was the lemon which was the object
of her attention, not the ice-cream.
I felt like intervening.
"Let the child have what she wants,"
I wanted to say.

The baby in the restaurant ....

"Can't you see the clear message she is giving you.
Will you not heed it.
Will you not let her have what she wants.
Must your will prevail over hers
in such a simple matter."
But I said nothing.
I didn't want to interfere.
However a deep sense of sadness arose within me.
Somehow in this simple scene,
I recognized what had happened
to me in my childhood.
If such loving and caring parents as these
were insensitive to the expressed needs
and wants of their child,
then what about all the other parents?
What about my parents?
What about your parents?
How much of my will and power
had been taken from me in such a simple way,
just because my parents didn't know any better.

The baby in the restaurant ....

No one had shown them
how to be fully present with a child.
No one had shown them how to be sensitive
to the expressed needs and wants of a child.
No one had told them how easy it was to
destroy the will and power of a young child
by excessively imposing their will upon the child.
As this lovely family got up to leave,
I could no longer restrain myself.
I told them that they had a beautiful child
and that I would write about her in my next book.
They were delighted.
"What is the baby's name?" I asked
"Sophia," replied the mother proudly.
"What does it mean?" I asked.
"Wisdom," she replied with a smile.
"Perfect!" I said with the strangest feeling
that the baby had quite knowingly
delivered this message to me.

The true child is a dimension of consciousness
just as the true mother and the true father
are dimensions of consciousness.

It is better to remain in a state of not knowing
than to go into the mind in search of an answer.

God has nothing to offer you
other than what is present
in this moment.

Gratitude is a blessing beyond measure.
It is a state of grace.
God responds to those who are truly grateful.

I am love.
I am truth.
I am beauty.
I am intelligence.
I am power.
I am.

Life is
profoundly
mysterious.
Relax.
Let go.
Surrender into the mystery.

Confusion

Confusion only arises
because you are trying to understand.
Surrender the need to understand
and confusion dissolves.
Only clarity remains
at the very heart of silence.

You came into this world without a name.
You will leave it without a name.
You exist in the moment.
You cannot be named.

The name game

We humans are the only species
to name everything we encounter.
The irony is that when we came
to name ourselves, we got it wrong.
We are not human Beings.
We are simply humans.
It is not until we awaken fully into the present
moment that we evolve into our name as Beings.
All the other species on the planet
are fully evolved in their Being.
A Gorilla Being.
A Donkey Being.
A Tree Being.
A Mosquito Being.
A Flower Being.
We have dishonored the true Beings
in our naming of them.

The name game ....

We have left the Being out of the naming process,
and we have misappropriated it for ourselves.
We are the only species on Earth
that have no right to use that word
in naming ourselves.
Certainly, the name indicates our potential.
It indicates our future.
Our destiny.
But we are not there yet.
We are the only ones not yet fully evolved.
We are the last to arrive.
And the sooner we realize it,
the sooner we will stop destroying those
who have arrived before us
with our arrogant illusion of superiority.
In our unconsciousness, we are causing great harm
to those who are more evolved than us.

If you are present, you cannot harm another.

If you want to act lovingly in the world,
then wash the dishes lovingly.

Forgiveness

Forgiveness is a useful way
to release the past,
but once the past is released,
you will see that there is nothing to forgive.

The forgiveness meditation

Close your eyes.
Bring yourself fully present
in your breathing body.
Bring yourself fully present with the sounds
you hear in this moment.
Relax into the silent presence of your Being.
And now take some time to reflect
back over your life.
Seek out the memory of all those
who have hurt you.
Begin with your mother.
She almost certainly has hurt you by not
giving you what you really wanted from her.
See her in front of you.
Make sure that she is attentive and then share
with her how she hurt you when you were a child.
Tell her what she did or failed to do that hurt you.
Tell her that she wasn't really there for you.
Tell her what you really wanted from her.
Tell her how it made you feel.
Tell her that you have been hurt and angry
for a long time.

The forgiveness meditation ....

Express the anger.
Allow the tears to flow if they want to.
Ask her if she would like your forgiveness.
And then forgive her.
Tell her that you release her from your past
and that she is no longer responsible for you.
Tell her that you are ready to take
full responsibility for yourself.
Tell her that you no longer blame her.
Tell her that you forgive her.
Thank her for any lessons she taught you
in the process of hurting you.
Find some words to complete
your communication with her.
You may want to express your love for her
but that is up to you.
And then let her go.
Allow her image to dissolve completely
as you become fully present once again.
Repeat the above process with your father
and then gradually work your way
through all the years and events of your life
forgiving all those people from your past
who may have hurt you.

The forgiveness meditation ....

You do not have to complete this in one sitting.
Take as long as you like.
When you have finished forgiving
all those who have hurt you,
repeat the whole process again, but this time
seeking out the memory of all those people
who might have been hurt by you.
Look back over your life and call up each person
from your past who you may have hurt either
intentionally or unintentionally.
Apologize!
Seek their forgiveness.
Release them from the past.
Ask them to release you.
If they refuse, then that is their freedom.
It is enough to know that if your apology
is true and sincere, then God will release you.
At the end of this process,
you will feel a sense of completion which will
allow you to release the past completely.
As the past is released, you will find it
so much easier to be fully present.
You will begin to enter into the truth of life.

To forgive is to release the past.
To release the past is to forgive.

If you are unable to forgive,
then you must still have
anger and blame repressed within you.
At an unconscious level,
you must be unwilling
to release the anger and the blame.
If there is no one left to blame,
then you will have to take
full responsibility for yourself.
You will have to take full responsibility
for your life as it is now.

The anger meditation

If you are carrying within you
a lot of repressed anger from the past,
it would be very wise to do the anger meditation
every day for at least a month.
After that you can do it as the need arises.
An anger meditation should last
about five or ten minutes.
Perfect expression of anger
is like playing the violin.
You must hit the right note.
It is not catharsis.
You are not trying to get rid of the anger.
Find the right tone of voice to express the anger.
Find the perfect facial expression to go with anger.
Clench you fists if you want to.
Beat a cushion if that helps.
It is best to be alone
so that no one gets caught up
in what you are saying.
And now let the meditation begin.

The anger meditation ....

Just allow the anger its full expression.
Be outrageous.
It is helpful to exaggerate anger's response.
Anger always wants to inflict a punishment
which is far greater than the crime.
Allow it to do so.
Blow up your mother with a hand grenade.
Throw your father into a pond full of crocodiles.
Be creative in getting even.
If after a while, you begin to laugh,
then know that you are expressing anger perfectly.
Anger is outrageous.
You are not meant to take it too seriously.
Express it.
Enjoy it.
Let it playfully explode within you.
Anger will set you free.

Completing the past.

What one sentence would you say
to your father to complete
your relationship with him?
What would hate say to him?
What would anger say to him?
What would rage say to him?
What would hurt say to him?
What would need say to him?
What would love say to him?
What one sentence would you say
to your mother to complete
your relationship with her?
What would hate say to her?
What would anger say to her?
What would rage say to her?
What would hurt say to her?
What would need say to her?
What would love say to her?

Self-abuse

Many people abuse themselves.
They are critical of themselves.
They are judgmental of themselves.
They get angry with themselves.
They have unreasonably high
expectations of themselves.
They put themselves down.
They blame themselves.
All these things are forms of self-abuse.
And if you pay close attention
to the words you use to abuse yourself,
you will see that they are not your words.
The words belong to your mother or father.
They said these things to you
when you were a child
in order to control you.
You were very hurt.
You were deeply wounded.

Self abuse ....

Eventually, you came to believe
that what they were saying must be true.
You took on your parent's words.
You took them into you.
And now you speak their words to yourself
as if you were their representative.
You have become their spokesperson.
You continue to speak their words
long after you have left home
and even long after they have died.
It is pointless to try to stop abusing yourself.
The very one trying to stop the abuse
is the one who is abusing.
It is like a house dividing against itself
and it will not work.
What will work is to come to a true decision
that you no longer want to abuse yourself.
You will no longer believe
in that script when it arises.

Self abuse ....

Do not try to stop the abuse
Simply recognize it as it arises
without any judgment.
"That was a little hard," you can say to yourself.
"I don't need to do that any more."
Or another time,
"I seem to be getting angry with myself.
I don't need to do that any more."
Or yet another time,
"I seem to be judging myself.
I don't need to do that any more."
You are not stopping the self abuse.
You are simply seeing it as it arises
and choosing not to follow it.
You are choosing not to believe in it.
You are choosing to be gentle on yourself.
You are choosing to be kind to yourself.

Don't be so hard on yourself.
Don't be so demanding of yourself.
Be gentle.
Be loving.
Be kind to yourself.

Don't diminish yourself in any way.
Dare to be all that you are.
Dare to be.

Criticism

Whenever someone criticizes you,
know that it is an attempt to belittle you.
It is an attempt to make you smaller
so that you can be more easily controlled.

Judgment

Judgment is more than an attempt to belittle you.
It is an attempt to annihilate you.
In truth, the only one annihilated
by judgment is the one judging.

There is nothing wrong with mind's world.
I am not against it in any way.
I have no judgment of mind's world.
It is just that it is not real.
It is an illusory world.
God's world is the world of here now.
Mind's world is the world of not here.
God's world is real.
Mind's world is not.

Thoughts and feelings

If thoughts are witnessed
by the consciousness of Being,
they will pass through you like thin white clouds
moving across a vast clear sky.
They will not accumulate within you.
If you personalize the thoughts,
by being for or against them in any way,
or by strongly believing in them,
then those thoughts will gather together
and form into a thick cloud cover,
so that not one ray of light
will be able to shine through.
Feelings are like a river.
They are meant to flow freely within you.
When you repress or deny your feelings,
you have dammed the river.
You have damned yourself.
Experience the feelings without thought.
Allow the feelings expression within you.
Allow the feelings to flow through you.
Do not be for or against the feelings in any way.
Just be like the banks of the river
as the river flows into the sea.

Awakening now

Awakening is immediate.
It is now or it is never.
It is always now or never.
And now is always presenting itself to you.
It never gives up on you.
Each new moment offers you
yet another opportunity to be present.
Moment to moment,
redemption is always available.

Becoming present

Look at something in front of you.
It could be a vase of flowers.
It could be a humble ashtray.
But it is present.
It is here.
It has more power to enlighten you
than all the spiritual books in the world.
Just tune in to the vase of flowers or the ashtray.
Become fully present with it.
If you are truly present with the flowers
or the ashtray, your thinking mind will fall silent.
You will become fully present.
In that moment of silent presence,
you are enlightened.
To be enlightened simply means
to be awake and fully present.
Moment to moment.

If you do not honor God
as the first priority and love in your life,
then you will never come to know God.

The first priority

The first priority in your life
has to be your own awakening.
God has to be number one in your life.
Relationship can be important to you.
Success can be important to you.
Earning money can be important to you.
It is just that God has to be number one.
Can you imagine God accepting less than that.
God will simply not respond to you.

Do not place your relationship with your loved ones
ahead of your relationship with God.

The path to God is a narrow path.
It must be walked in single file.
You must go to God alone.

Relationship

Relationship is one of the most
complex and difficult issues to integrate
into the process of awakening.
Relationship by its very nature exists within time.
It will inevitably take you into the mind.
And when you are in the mind, all the unresolved
issues of your childhood relationship with
your mother and father will come flooding in.
The inner child will miraculously come to life
and project its wounded reality onto
your current relationships.
Like a magician, you conjure up the past
with all its unfulfilled needs,
hurt, resentment and anger,
which are then projected onto the present,
thereby damaging or destroying
the relationship which you are now in.
If you want to avoid this, you will have to place the
emphasis not on relationship, but on relatedness.

Relationship ....

Relatedness occurs in the present moment.
You can only experience relatedness
when you are present.
It is relatedness which brings
intimacy into your life.
Only when you are truly present with each other
will you feel nourished and supported.
Many people are together without ever
being truly present with each other.
They are just using each other
to avoid the pain of aloneness.
And yet they still feel the pain.
They cannot escape from it.
Learn how to be present.
Let relatedness in the present moment
be the foundation of your life together.
Do not take each other for granted.
You do not need to know
what the future brings.
Just enjoy all that the present moment
has to offer you.

Most people enter relationship
to avoid their aloneness.

When you are in a relationship,
do not have the sense that your partner
helps you to escape your aloneness.
Rather, have the sense that your partner
supports you in your aloneness.

The value of relationship

There are two reasons for being in a relationship.
The first is the most common.
Relationship is extremely effective
in revealing all those things about yourself
which you would rather not see.
If you are willing to open your eyes
and look into the mirror of your relationship,
you will begin to see all the unconscious patterns
of control, judgment, inadequacy, blame, guilt,
need, expectation, manipulation, helplessness,
unworthiness, isolation and fear which were
programmed into your mind during your early
childhood relationship with your parents.

The value of relationship ....

To bring consciousness to these patterns is
an essential part of the awakening process.
This kind of relationship usually begins with
falling in love and often ends in the divorce courts.
There is another kind of relationship
which is possible.
Once you have awakened, there is no greater joy
than sharing the present moment with another
who is also present.
This kind of relationship is based on relatedness
in the present moment rather than having someone
meet your unfulfilled needs from the past or
provide you with a guarantee of security
in the future.
Be very grateful to those who can enter
into this kind of relationship with you.

The eternal dilemma of man and woman

From the woman's perspective,
her eternal dilemma is that the man
is never fully present with her.
He never gives of himself fully.
And so she feels used.
She feels cheated.
She feels dishonored.
She feels unsatisfied.
She refuses to let go of him
until he is fully present with her.
She will cling to him.
She will manipulate him.
She will interfere with him.
She will destroy him if she has to.
But she will not let him go
until he is fully present with her.
From the man's perspective,
he will not be fully present with her
because he knows that she will not let him go.
She will not release him.
And he must be released.

The eternal dilemma of man and woman ....

It is a kind of death for him if he is not released.
The eternal dilemma of man and woman
is like the chicken and the egg.
Which comes first?
She will not release him
because he is not fully present.
He will not be fully present
because she will not release him.
This eternal dilemma is deeply entrenched
into their relationship with each other.
It will never change until
man and woman reach an agreement.
He will have to agree to be fully present with her.
And she will have to agree to release him fully.
The release is a phenomenon of consciousness.
It is an acknowledgment that each of us is One.
Not two.
Man and woman ought not
to think of themselves as a couple.

The eternal dilemma of man and woman ....

They are individuals choosing
to share a loving life together.
Man is One.
Woman is One.
One and One do not make two.
They make One.
If you allow One and One to make two,
then you destroy the One.
I am not saying that when the man is released
he will leave the woman.
I am not saying that he will use her
and then leave her.
In a perfectly evolved world,
man and woman will live together
as divine husband and wife.
He will want to share a loving life with her.
In her he finds a true and constant companion.
He is always fully present when he is with her.
She never clings to him or holds on to him.
She is secure within herself.

The eternal dilemma of man and woman ....

She feels honored and recognized by him.
She is satisfied.
They relate to each other with love and true caring.
They do not attempt to interfere with each other.
They are fully present with each other.
They allow a natural flow
to evolve within their relationship.
Just like the tides of the sea,
they come together and separate
harmoniously and naturally
many times during the day and night.
But when they do come together,
they are fully present with each other.
And when they separate, it is a true letting go.
Each one moves into the next moment
without clinging to the moment
which has just past.
This kind of relationship is our destiny.
It is our true future.
Until now, we have got it wrong.
It is time to start again.

As we awaken

As we awaken into Being,
we will begin to recognize each other.
I will see you as a Being of love.
You will see me as a Being of love.
We will not need anything from each other
apart from the gift of being present
with each other.
For each of us is complete and whole.
We can share in a loving energy.
We can share the moment together.
And if we share enough loving moments together,
then we will be sharing a loving life together.

Woman

Woman, you are a divine Being of love.
Your body is sacred.
It is better to be alone and celibate
than to be used as a sexual object
by an unconscious man
who does not know
who you are.

Woman has never really left God.
It is man whose nature it is to come and go.

Nourishing ourselves

We are nourished by being present.
We can be present with a tree or a flower
or we can be present with another human being.
When we are truly present,
we are nourished by the presence
of everything around us.

If you feel depleted in energy,
go outside and become fully present with a tree.
Have the sense that you are drawing into yourself
the silent presence of the tree.
The presence of the tree will fill you.
It will restore you.
It will make you strong.
It is wise to first ask the tree's permission
if you may fill yourself in this way.

God does not exist in the mind.
You will have to come out of the mind
if you are to honor the truth of God
in the present moment.

The present moment

The present moment
is always calling for your attention.
Just look and you will see.
Each leaf moving in the breeze
is waving to you.
It is saying,
"Here I am.
Will you not be present with me?
Will you not see me?"
Each flower is trying to attract you
with its colour and its beauty.
"What more can I do?" asks the flower.
"Will you not see me?
Will you not be present with me.
Do you not know who I am.
I am God in the form of a flower.
And I am trying to attract your attention."

Is this moment enough?

God has nothing more to offer you
than that which is present in the moment.
Is it enough for you?
God wants to know!
Because if it is not enough for you,
then you will have to leave
the present moment.
You will have to enter
the illusory world of the mind
in search of something more.

The Quest

A man was searching for the key to happiness.
One day he came upon a sage
sitting by the side of the road.
"Where can I find happiness?" asked the man.
"It is here," answered the sage.
The man looked around.
"But there is nothing here," he said.
"There is nothing here," answered the sage,
"because you are not here. How can you know
what is here if you are not here?"
The man looked confused.
"Become fully present with the trees," said the sage.
"Become fully present with the flowers
and the birds and the distant mountain."
Guided by the sage, the man was able
to bring himself fully present, and as he did so,
everything began to change.
The trees became vibrant and alive.
They were full of light.
They seemed eternal.
The flowers exploded into all the colors
of the rainbow.
The song of the birds filled the man's ears.
He could feel the soft caress
of the breeze upon his face.
And he was warmed gently by the sun.
He began to feel extremely calm and peaceful.

The Quest ....

His mind was completely still.
Not a single thought arose.
He felt love arising within him.
He felt a sense of oneness and perfection
arising within him.
He was in ecstasy and bliss.
A sense of inner knowing filled him
and at last he was at peace.
For the first time in his life he felt full within.
And he was very, very happy.
Just then he heard a voice inside of him.
It was the voice of his mind.
It was the voice of his ego.
"Do not listen to this foolish old man!" said the
voice. "What can he offer you? Just a few trees,
some flowers and the distant mountain. That is
nothing. I can offer you so much more.
I can offer you everything. All you have to do is
think, and it is yours. All you have to do is
imagine and I will take you there. I can promise
you all the treasures of the world. I can promise
you fame and power and glory. Ask this so called
sage if he can offer you that?"
The sage shook his head.
"I can offer you all the knowledge of the past"
said the voice."Ask the sage if he can offer
you that."

The Quest ....

The sage shook his head.
"I can promise you a better future," said the voice.
"Ask the sage if he can do that?"
The sage shook his head.
"I can bring you everything that is missing in your
life. I can fix up everything that is wrong. Ask the
sage if he can do that!"
The sage shook his head.
The man had heard enough.
"What can you offer me?" he asked the sage.
"Only what is present in this moment,"
answered the sage.
"Is that all?" asked the man.
"Nothing more than that." said the sage.
The man thought for a while.
"No contest!" said the voice triumphantly
inside the man's head. "No contest!"
"There is nothing here," said the man. "Just a few
trees, some flowers and the distant mountain."
With that the man continued on his way,
in pursuit of that which his mind
had promised him.
The sage watched as the man
disappeared down the road.
"No contest," said the sage to the trees
and the flowers and the distant mountain.
"No contest."

The only thing I trust is silence.
And I trust silence completely.

The ultimate truth
is the silent presence of God.
Whatever reveals itself
through the silent presence
is the truth of God.

In silence the truth is known

To agree or to disagree
with what I am saying
has nothing to do
with the truth.
It is your mind which agrees or disagrees
and your mind can never know the truth.
When you are fully present,
there is no agreement.
There is no disagreement.
There is only silence.
And in silence the truth is known.

Out of the Silence

Find the voice of your Being.
It will arise out of the silence.
Find that inner place of knowing.
It is at the very heart of the silence.

Offer your prayers into the silence

Offer your prayers into the silence.
Offer your questions into the silence.
Offer your love and gratitude into the silence.
And always allow whatever arises
out of the silence to return to silence.
Always return to God what is God's.

The more you live in gratitude for what you have,
the more you will have to be grateful for.

When at last you emerge
from the maze of the mind,
you will be a-mazed.

Entering the mystery

Once you awaken into the present moment,
you will begin to recognize the mystery of life.
You will begin to see that God is present
and deeply involved in every moment of your life.

Trust in God

Every leaf falling from every tree
is falling at exactly the time
and in exactly the way
that God planned.
Watch a leaf fall.
Its journey to the ground
has been planned by God
in perfect detail.
Every movement in the wind,
every change in direction,
every floating,
flying
falling
movement
is pre-determined by God
in perfect detail
long before
the tree
itself
came
into
existence.
If God has such a perfect plan
for the journey of a leaf from a tree,
how much more perfect is God's plan for you.

A mystic is one who has entered
into the mystery of existence.
A mystic is one who is willing to allow
existence to remain a mystery.

Everything in physical existence
is the Body of God.
Bring yourself present and you will find yourself
in the Body of God.
Bring yourself present and you will find yourself
in the Garden of Eden.

The ego does not want you to wake up

The ego does not want you to wake up.
It will pretend that it wants you to wake up.
It will have you reading every spiritual book
and following every spiritual path
and visiting every spiritual teacher.
It wants to become more spiritual.
But if you do happen to stumble upon the truth,
so that there is a very real possibility
of your full awakening, the mind will have
you looking elsewhere almost immediately.
It does not want you to wake up because if you
awaken, it will no longer be in control of you.
It will no longer be in charge.
If the true master appears,
the ego will have to vacate the throne.

When you awaken, you are the true master.
But only of yourself.

I am an earthquake.
I am here to disturb your beliefs.
I am here to shake you up
and cause a crack to appear
in the unshakable world
of your illusions.

Time means nothing to God.

God wants you here.
You can only be of service to God
when you are fully present.

In between the words I speak,
there is nothing.
If you pay attention
to the space
between my words
and to the pauses
between the sentences,
you will see that there is nothing there.
There is nothing behind the words.
There is no one behind the words.

There is only one Being.
We are all individual expressions
of the one Being.

In truth,
I am you
posing as me.

When you bring the consciousness of Being
to the mind, you take away from the mind
its power and ability to deceive you
and control you.

There is only one mind.
Once you know your own mind,
you know all minds.

That which is to come is already past.
That which is past is yet to come.

The end is contained within the beginning.
The beginning is contained within the end.
Both the beginning and the end are here now.

The true future unfolds
through the present moment.
It can only unfold through
the present moment.

If you are not present, then it is the past
which projects forward and poses as the future.
It prevents the true future from unfolding.

As you become more and more present,
an evolved dimension of yourself
from your own future
will begin to emerge
through the doorway
of the present moment.
As you become more present,
you will begin to encounter
your future self.
Who you have been
and who you will be
meet and merge
and become One
in the sanctity
of the present moment.

You are the Saviour
but only of yourself.
To save yourself
simply means to awaken
out of the past and future
into the present moment.

Love and beauty

The experience of beauty
has been a profound
and powerful part of my journey.
Beauty and love are so closely related
that it is impossible to experience one
without experiencing the other.

I am not attached

I am not attached
to any experience from the past.
Not even the experience of Heaven on Earth.

Neither for nor against anything,
I simply am.

God is without judgment.

Judgment

As long as you continue to judge,
you will be denied entry into God's world,
not because you have done anything wrong,
not because you are evil,
but simply because judgment
is incompatible with the true nature of God.

The original sin is judgment.

Adam and Eve

In Genesis, we are told that Adam and Eve
were ejected from the Garden of Eden
because they had eaten of the fruit of the tree
of knowledge of what is good and evil.
To decide what is good and evil is a judgment.
It is judgment that resulted in the ejection
of Adam and Eve from the Garden of Eden.
It is judgment that prevents their return.
God had warned them against judgment.
Now judgment had taken them
into the world of duality.
It had taken them out of the Mind of God
into a world of their own minds.
They had chosen to separate from God
and go their own way.
Now they are condemned to live in a world
of their own creation.
Adam and Eve exist within each one of us.
It is a story which reflects
our original state of consciousness.
It reflects our original state of Being.
We began in the Garden of Eden.
We began in a state of innocence.
We began in the Mind of God.
Now we are separated from God.

Adam and Eve ....

We are fallen from God and the only thing
which keeps us fallen is our continuing judgment.
When we come to recognize that judgment
is the original sin that led us astray,
we can begin the long and delicate process
of transcending judgment in our lives.
When we have transcended judgment completely,
we will find that we have been restored to God.
We have been returned to the Garden of Eden.
We have found our way home.
But to our utter amazement we will find
that the Garden of Eden no longer exists
within the mind of God.
That which began as an image in the mind of God
has been manifested into physical form.
The Mind of God has given birth
to the Body of God.
The Garden of Eden now exists in physical form.
It is our planet Earth.
When we awaken fully into the present moment,
we will realize that we have come home.
In fact, we have always been home.
But like Adam and Eve, we have abandoned God
and the Garden of Eden by journeying into the
illusory world of our own minds.

Beyond judgment

The only way
to go beyond judgment
is to witness yourself judging.
Do not try to stop judgment,
for that too would be a judgment.
It would be a judgment of judgment.
Just see judgment as it arises within you.
Own it.
Confess it.
Express it.
Allow judgment to exist within you
but do not believe in it.
Judgment is waiting to be accepted.
It is the final test.
Once you pass the test,
judgment will release you.

The Judge

Explore the Judge within you.
Let judgment arise within you.
Own judgment within you.
Take full responsibility for judgment.
Become Judgment itself.
Bring Judgment into the full
light of consciousness.
God will love you for it.

Beyond judgment

If you want to go beyond judgment,
then you will have to get to know judgment.
Know yourself as the one who judges.
Know yourself as the one who is judged.
Witness judgment in its many forms.
Witness judgment in its many disguises.
Witness judgment each time it arises in your life.
As you come to know judgment
and as you accept it without judgment,
it will begin to dissolve.
It will disappear from your life completely.
You will experience a life without judgment.

No one is guilty.

Not knowing is the doorway to knowing.

Knowing arises out of silence.
It arises out of the present moment.
If you allow it to return to silence,
then you remain innocent.
One who is innocent
is one who is willing to remain
in a state of not knowing.

The way is simple

The way is simple.
Be here now.
Transcend judgment.
Bring yourself into balance within duality.
Surrender fear and control.
Live in true responsibility.
Accept and acknowledge the many aspects
and dimensions of yourself particularly
at the level of ego.
Be in right relationship with yourself.
Be in right relationship with others.
Be in right relationship with your feelings.
Be in right relationship with life.
Be in right relationship with God.
Act lovingly in the world.
Be a light unto yourself.
Be a light unto the world.

Communion with Truth

The only way you can come into communion
with the truth is in silence.
The thinking mind can never know the truth.
If you try to place what I am saying
into the framework of your existing understanding
then you will destroy the truth.
You will have stolen the truth from silence
and given it to the mind to use.

Just being present will heal you.
It will heal the wounds and traumas of the past.
You do not have to do anything.
Just trust that when you are present,
God is present within you.
Trust that God knows what to do.

To be present is to be whole.
To be whole is to be healed.

The present moment never leaves you.
It is you who leaves the present moment.

The ego has been sitting in the throne of God.
It is up to the ego to see that it is an imposter.
It must surrender of its own choice.

Once you have awakened
to the dimension of Being,
then God will do the work for you.
Relax. Trust. Surrender.
God knows what God is doing.

You don't have to be present all the time

You don't have to be present all the time
to live an awakened life.
As long as you are grounded
in the reality of the present moment
it is perfectly appropriate and safe
to enter the mind and the world of time.
It would be very difficult to live in the world
as it is now without entering the mind.
Someone has to fill out the tax returns.
Someone has to remember the next
appointment with the dentist.
Without the mind and its capacity
for remembering, you would be unable
to perform the simplest of tasks.
You would not even know your name.
As long as you know that the truth of life
exists solely in the present moment, you are free
to enter into the illusory world of the mind at will.
I would suggest, however that you restrict
each journey into the mind to a maximum
duration of two hours.

You don't have to be present all the time ....

At work, you can enter fully into the thinking
world of the mind in order to function effectively.
But take a break.
Come out of the mind at regular intervals
and reconnect to the truth and reality
of the present moment.
Become present with the pot plant
standing patiently in the corner.
Become present with the pen lying
on the desk in front of you.
Become present with the sound of voices
emanating from the next office.
By becoming present with that which is actually
here now, you will bring yourself out of the mind
into the truth and reality of the present moment.
Entering into the mind
is like a journey into space.
It is wise to stay connected with home base.
Otherwise you might get lost.
You might not be able to find your way home.

Surrendering to God

To become fully present is like bringing yourself
to the door of God and saying to God
"I am here.
I give myself to you.
I am surrendered.
Do with me as you will!"

God's law

"Not in your time, but in My time.
Not on your terms, but on My terms.
Not your way but My way."
This is an expression of God's law.
It is God's declaration to each one of us.

I can use you

"I can use you but you cannot use me."
This is another statement by God to each one of us.
It is another one of God's laws.
The human mind or ego is always seeking
to gain an advantage for itself in some way.
In the pursuit of enlightenment,
you may be subtly seeking
to empower yourself over others.
You may be seeking to glorify yourself.
You may be unconsciously hoping to use
the truth of God to advance yourself in some way.
You may even get away with it for a while.
You may gain some degree of fame or recognition.
But sooner or later,
you will have to learn your lesson.
You cannot use God or the truth of God.
It is God who will use you.
Wait.
Be patient.
God's plan will be revealed to you.
It will be revealed through the events
and circumstances unfolding in your life.
Ultimately your awakening is not for you.
It is for all those who have not yet awakened.

When you fully awaken
then the mind will be
your loving and devoted servant,
just as you will be a loving
and devoted servant of God.
If you do not serve God,
then the mind will not serve you.
You have a choice.
Either God is your Master.
Or your mind will be your Master.
It is up to you.

ABOUT THE AUTHOR

Leonard Jacobson is a modern mystic and leading spiritual teacher who is deeply committed to guiding and supporting others in their journey towards wholeness. He was born in Melbourne, Australia in 1944 and educated at the University of Melbourne, graduating in law in 1969. He practiced law until 1979.

He then he set off on a long journey of spiritual discovery which took him all over the world, from the United States to the Middle East, India, and Japan. In 1981, he experienced the first of a series of spontaneous mystical awakenings which profoundly altered his perception of life, truth and reality. Each of these experiences took him to deeper and deeper levels of consciousness.

He has been running workshops and seminars for the past sixteen years, offering inspiration and guidance to those on the path of awakening. His teachings and his presence are a powerful reminder that the source of life and truth is within each one of us.

He now lives in the USA and returns to Australia regularly. He offers a comprehensive program of private and telephone sessions, evening and one day seminars, weekend workshops and longer retreats. To find out when there will be a seminar in your local area or to order books and tapes by Leonard Jacobson or to schedule a telephone session, call 1-888-367-3315 (toll-free) or visit the author's web site at www.leonardjacobson.com.

In Australia, write to Leonard Jacobson Seminars, PO Box 434, Byron Bay, NSW 2481, Australia.

Words from Silence

An Invitation to Spiritual Awakening

This powerful book reveals many of the hidden keys to awakening, offering clear guidance to those on a spiritual path. Each page is a lyrically beautiful expression of an essential truth. Zen-like in its simplicity, it communicates directly with the heart and soul of the reader, gently inviting a response from the deepest level of Being.

ISBN 1-890580-00-7, 256 pages
Available from leading book stores.
To order a copy of *Words from Silence*
call 1-888-367-3315
or visit the author's website at
www.leonardjacobson.com

Bridging Heaven & Earth

A Return to the One

This book provides insight and understanding, which arise from the deepest levels of enlightenment. It covers such diverse topics as the multi-dimensional nature of our existence, the eternal dilemma of God, the soul's journey, healing the soul, the descent of Spirit, keys to awakening, liberation from the ego, the Universal laws of life, God consciousness, the truth about Jesus. And so much more.

ISBN 1-890580-02-3, 288 pages
Available from leading book stores.
To order a copy of *Bridging Heaven & Earth*
call 1-888-367-3315
or visit the author's website at
www.leonardjacobson.com

Leonard Jacobson

To find out when there will be a seminar in your local area or to order books and tapes or to schedule a telephone session:

In the USA, call 1-888-367-3315 (toll free)

In Australia, write to Leonard Jacobson Seminars, PO Box 434, Byron Bay, NSW 2481, Australia.

**Visit the author's website:
www.leonardjacobson.com**